How to Jump from a Moving Train

Oriana Ivy

Červená Barva Press
Somerville, Massachusetts

Červená Barva Press
P.O. Box 440357
W. Somerville, MA 02144-3222

www.cervenabarvapress.com

Bookstore: www.thelostbookshelf.com

Cover Art: "Crossing the River Styx" Joachim Patinir
(circa 1480–1524)

Cover design: William J. Kelle

ISBN: 978-1-950063-65-9

ACKNOWLEDGMENTS

Charon's Gift: *Blue Fifth Review*

My Mother Shows Me the Human Brain: *Texas Review*

My Mother Asks Me Not to Write: *Los Angeles Review*

My Mother Is Prepared: *Poetry*

Azure: *Tidepools*

TABLE OF CONTENTS

How to Jump from a Moving Train

CHARON'S GIFT

My father-in-law from the country of the dead
sends me a gift, my inheritance:
an envelope stuffed with banknotes,
and a purse burdened with coins.

The banknotes rustle in sepia
scrolled in Cyrillic alphabet.
Maybe it's Tzarist rubles,
or money from beyond

the ghetto of time. See, he gives it back:
his passage to America,
the slaughterhouses of Chicago.

I weigh the purse in my hands,
afraid to look inside:
whose face
will be on those coins?

Still the coins should be worth
the trouble of dying —
even the coppers dropped
in the blind pools of beggars' caps.

*

Pa, the old miser, starting with a crate
of horseradish hawked
on a street corner in Milwaukee —
From his butcher shop he kept

the tall white scale to weigh the souls.
Those too heavy with regret

are hung from meat hooks to forget
that yellowed bundle of love letters

before they married someone else.
Those too light from the belief
that life is but a joke, a dream,
are pressed with stone like sauerkraut.

With frost-red fingers he taps the coins:
"The best deal in town —
you can have these for a song,"
he says, hoarder and herder,

his voice cracked
with millennia of hardship
and drink, worn out
with the passage from shore to shore.

But whose face
is on those coins?
Everyone's, he says,
everyone's.

MY MOTHER SHOWS ME THE HUMAN BRAIN
Nencki Institute of Experimental Biology, Warsaw

She rushes home with a miracle.
Puts it on the table: *This is a human brain* —
trembling on the metal tray, the color of
wet clay, webbed with tattered membranes.

Mother nudges it with a glass rod:
here lay the valley of speech,
the relay stations of hearing.
Here curled the beginning of memory,

near hunger and smell and fear.
Here used to wake someone's world,
folded into the tender
white-gray neural ravines.

*

Cat and goat brains are the daily brain.
Hypothalamus is a household word.
I hardly notice, but a friend
almost fainted once

when Mother passed through the room
in a white coat,
carrying a brain-cutting saw
like an avenging angel.

I like the Gothic armature of labs,
the dark hush, the red warning lamps.
Oscillographs click, spinning green
sinusoids. Sagittal cross-sections

gleam among our groceries,
behind the steel claws of cold storage.

I sit on the windowsill,
four flights above sad Warsaw,

blessing flat Socialist rooftops:
Septum — amygdala —nucleus caudatus.

*

*In nature there is nothing
supernatural,* she says as I
leaf through foreign
neurology journals. My neurons

fire in a nervous scribble,
my relays create the world.
By definition,
she adds while I tremble

between definitions,
waiting to become
a butterfly, methyl blue,
pinned in the heaven of science.

CONNECTIONS

"I saw *Babcia* in a dream," mother tells me.
"She stood in the kitchen and said,
Make a wish — because I have
connections everywhere."

But my mother had forgotten
all her wishes like a flustered little girl.
The temptation, to believe our dead
have connections everywhere

and could pull some cosmic strings.
But those strings had already been pulled
when I had the mother I had.
Our first Thanksgiving in Los Angeles,

she divided our one turkey TV dinner,
choosing the smaller portion, as always,
for herself. She said, *The only real*
poverty is here — and touched her head.

A FAILED PROPAGANDA MEETING
AT CINEMA DESIRE

Since earliest childhood we were told
the red in the Polish flag stood for blood.
Now on the stage, two colossal

bouquets of red gladioli.
In the haze of upward petals,
the balding propagandist blossoms:

Isn't the Soviet Union
the greatest, the most advanced,
the most democratic country in the world?

He raises his voice: "Let us
salute our brother: *Long live
the Soviet Union*!" He lifts his arms

like an orchestra conductor,
motioning us to respond with a choral
Long live! I move my lips

in a mute shout,
raising my chin to mime
the final vowel like a howl.

Long live! the political educator
strains at the top of his amplified voice —
along with a squeak

of a few voices from the front row.
I look around: my classmates are
moving their lips without making a sound.

The theater is filled with classes
from several schools —
more than three hundred students.

The propagandist shouts even louder,
Long live the Soviet Union!
Again the sweeping motion of his arms.

This time a stumbling chorus
of six or seven voices.
Once more the educator tries

to rouse us to the correct zeal —
then shrugs — then strides —
then breaks into a run

toward the side door.
The wind of his retreat
barely musses the heavy gladioli.

BUS, TIJUANA, MEXICO

Odd, how at home I feel
in this ramshackle Tijuana bus
that slouches at the chipped curb,
La vida eterna

advertised on its side.
I could afford a taxi, but no,
I want this wooden seat,
this is third class, I'm loving it.

I only wish there'd be a live chicken
on this bus, it's not the same
without an animal soul.
I sit on the hard seat

knowing there is no hurry,
most of the world is like this —
no need to scribble false cheer
in letters home, or get another degree.

The bus is a church, with pews,
Our Lady of the Sorrows
on the dashboard, the driver
a rough-hewn apostle.

The kingdom will be his, why rush?
After a long snorting warm-up,
we start toward the U.S. border.
I'm going to America again,

where I will be poor
and will have to drive —
where I will have to take my life
in my own small hands.

OUR LADY OF THE THIRD ARM

17th-century icon, Moscow; Timken Gallery, San Diego

Because you need two arms
to be a woman,
and one to pick the fruit
from the Tree of Life.

Two to do cooking and laundry,
the third one to conduct
an orchestra of clouds.
Two to type, and the other one
to embroider the handkerchief of time.

The museum says the third arm
was painted in after the theft
of a votive offering made
by Saint John of Damascus.

Legends lie. Women know. Three
is the minimum design:
two to pick up a crying child,
and the third one to embrace yourself.

It's the worst handicap,
not having the third arm,
the one that grows in solitude —
the one that gathers twilight

and the birds' last chorale.
The one that waves goodbye,
while the other two
are still serving food to the guests.

Our Lady in her crown of stars
is busy holding the divine —
but with her stolen third arm
she blesses us
from a golden Byzantine sky.

MY MOTHER ASKS ME NOT TO WRITE
ABOUT WWII

"Why write about this old stuff?"
Not for this she gave me life.
Not for this she sent me
to the country of the future.

"Hitler is dead," she says.
She remembers that night —
The chill, uncertain May
has just begun. She's not in

ruined Warsaw, but in her leafy
home town, sleeping,
when church bells wake her up,
ringing loud and wild.

Lights go on in the windows,
people rush into streets,
women in coats over nightgowns
moon-shadowed, glancing,

whispering. Someone shouts:
"Hey, these are wedding bells!"
A few men run back in
to listen to the radio —

the Red Army entered
Hitler's bunker, found
two bodies partly burned:
Hitler and Eva Braun.

The bells sway the stunned air.
Neighbors and strangers
embrace, kiss on both cheeks,
laugh and weep. *Hitler is*

dead, is dead, is dead,
the bells ring until everyone's heard,
and the difficult future begins —
wedding bells in the dark.

LIVING IN THE ZOO
Poznań, 1945-46

The first year after the war,
one third of the city destroyed,
my mother was lucky to get a room
in the Pavilion of Small Mammals.

Her best friend was a mongoose.
Now and then she'd bring him a rare
delicacy, an egg. He'd cup it in his paws,
cut two dainty holes with his teeth
and suck out the contents.

She woke to the roaring of lions.
The hippopotamus mooed
for his cartload of wilted leaves;
Three owls like Fates turned parallel
heads as she passed. Llamas spat at her.
The toucans side-stepped on the branches
of their one pruned elm.

Early autumn Soviet soldiers arrived,
the third wave returning from Berlin.
They broke twigs from the trees
to poke at the animals.
The hippopotamus hid in his pond.
My mother saw the tiny bumps
where his nostrils wrinkled the dark water.

The biggest drama starred the elephant,
bought ten years earlier from a circus keeper:
"A bad animal, difficult to train."
Now the circus again came to town.

The circus keeper entered the enclosure:
"That's my old buddy —

I know how to handle him."
Moments later the enraged elephant
hurled his former master
over the fence onto the cement.

The zoo director's breath steamed with vodka,
but he knew every single animal.
He sported long whiskers;
colleagues joked that the director spent
so much time with the animals,
he had grown to resemble a seal.
His show-off act was to walk
into the lion cage and pat
the male lion on the behind.

His favorite was the giraffe he'd brought
after the war from another zoo.
A low trolley was built,
a rope fastened around the giraffe's neck;
two people pulled it down when the truck
approached an overpass or a tunnel.

In her new home, every day
the director went to see the giraffe.
She thrived. Then her legs got swollen,
she could only kneel. One day she lay down.
The director embraced her neck, and wept.
The giraffe died in his arms.

My father visited my mother
when she lived in the zoo.
She left the town to marry him.
The three owls lit her way
with the lanterns of their eyes.
The toucans stood, an orange dawn
in the branches of their wrong tree.

MY MOTHER IS PREPARED

Once at a party someone asked:
"What would you take
if World War III began,
and you headed for the hills?"
Incurable intellectuals, we all

named favorite books, except for one
psychology professor who sighed,
"Some quick, painless means
to commit suicide." My mother said,
"First, you need a warm blanket."

The guests fell still — then chatted again
about movies and vacations.
Nobody mentioned
the railroad platform in Kraków,
last chance to be bribed out of Auschwitz.

The window stippled with ghost drizzle,
rain turning to fine snow.
"They don't understand
anything," she whispered to me
in Polish, kissing me good-bye.

HOW TO JUMP FROM A MOVING TRAIN

Backwards. If you jump forward,
you'll be sucked down under the wheels.
Backwards, blindly, rolled into a ball,
hands cradling the back of your neck.

Note the terrain where you'll be thrust
away from the speeding locomotive.
On a soft meadow, you might get up;
on hard gravel, you'll break your bones.

I'm doomed to carry these instructions
in the planet of my skull, memory's
mass grave. After meeting someone new,
why do I think, "She could hide me"?

Why did I shudder when a Buddhist monk
said, "There is no doubt: in your past life,
you died at Auschwitz." Now I know
it's enough to be a child of survivors,

to whose cunning and blind luck I owe
my life. But an old movie is bleeding
through, of jumping backwards, away
from the transport — half-broken

crawling on sharp gravel
until the sheltering trees — until
water, food, cool wind toward
the springtime of my birth. Forward.

SURPRISED BY MY OWN BREASTS

Suicide fantasies — last night I had them
like a meteor shower. Too late,
I thought: I should have done it

the time I stood with a Polish artist
on the roof of an abandoned factory.
I saw the leap, I saw

my body falling — falling —
onto the grimy street below,
a wino sleeping under cardboard,

the desolation of America
pulling me down like gravity.
He called me by my childhood

name, its three clear vowels
a Baltic seagull against
the polluted Los Angeles sky. Why

couldn't I respond? Was it the year
I threw myself at an alcoholic
Vietnam veteran? I already was

a fallen woman, might as well
sleep with artists. Eros has
a twin brother, the one lover

who will never leave you —
one who kisses like the wind,
one who whispers: Die. Leap

into the night and shatter
in a million stars.

*

But in the morning when I woke up
I was surprised by my own breasts —
as if I saw them for the first time,

soft and female and defenseless,
the nipples like wild strawberries.
Why have we been of little use,

they seemed to ask, aren't we sweet?
Warm from sleep, in tendrils
of morning light, my body

waited. I'll keep you, I nodded
to my breasts.

HALLOWEEN BIRCHES

Moonlight was silvering
the palm tree on my lawn.
It lit up the long arc of one frond.

After many years in California,
my first thought: A weeping birch?
I have a birch tree on my lawn?

And birch groves left behind a lifetime
ago came to me, bowed and flowed —
cloudy branches of that Celtic night

when the blindfold of time slips loose
and we see behind and beyond —
just as now that I can barely walk,

memories of mountain hikes
clamber to my mind: Angel's Landing,
Never Summer, Dead Man's Pass.

Surprised by the brilliant crescent,
I walked on. The last of Halloween
children dressed as flame-red

devilkins or pink ballerina angels
were shooed by mothers into cars.
Only the souls of trees walked with me —

birches and beeches, maples, pines.
I whispered to them: *Remember me.*
They replied: *It's not important to be*

remembered — only to be beautiful.
The moon swam in the sky, a slender
canoe: *Get in, and not later but now.*

AZURE

We stood on the cliffs.
She was eighty then.
The spray leapt,
a shimmering prayer.

The ocean was showing off
its best blue. She turned to me
in triumph. *Azure,*
she said like a child

at the beginning of language.
Azure, she repeated
like a scientist, having classified
the degree of this infinity.

Luminous
from the sea, she handed it to me,
that marine mother hue,
the blue syllable of love —

the miracle mothers perform,
giving us the world
and the word. And the flaming
wheel passes on.

MOTHER MOON

I tuck a baby blanket
around her shrunken body,
wheel her past the patients parked
in wheelchairs against the wall —

the fractured elders sent to this
"Rehab Center" to be trained
to walk again, though they don't see
what there is to walk to.

In the patio, sharp breath of February wind,
the dry rasp of banana leaves.
"Cold," she shivers. I tuck her tight
in her pink cocoon of hearts and balloons.

She looks up at the sky
and smiles. "Moon," she says,
her face in that moment
again her own,

not a stiffening mask.
In the pale heaven over Los Angeles,
a frail daytime moon
hangs like an unfinished watercolor.

Earlier that week a baby girl I know
pointed with her finger and said
"moon" for the first time.
My mother pulls one finger

from under the blanket
and points up. "Moon,"
she says for the last time,
her eyes blossoming with light.

LAST WORDS

Don't kneel before the enemy!
she calls after me, loud,
slipping into the twilight
of that motto in our family,
going back to the days of the Tzar.

I shrug: how archaic
my mother has become,
marble as the moon,
dissolving like a cloud. But who
was my enemy? Those who'd destroy

what in me was different, wild?
Old pigeons on memory's windowsill,
gray and huddled now. Yet there was
an enemy inside. I knew him
and I loved him: the spirit that says No.

Rilke wrote: Life always says
both No and Yes. Death alone
says only Yes. When I was
seventeen my spirit said Yes,
and the homeless voyages that followed

taught me that Pacific sunsets
were enough. I wanted to travel easy
in the comfort of my mind.
But a difficult blessing
has been passed on to me:

In the name of the Mother,
the Daughter, and the Holy Ghost
of Not Giving Up.

WHITNEY PORTAL

What she loved was the view
of the highest peak —
the mountain's two great wings,
a granite angel. Silent strokes

were eroding the trails
in my mother's brain. I thought,
if only she could live
in a nursing home in Lone Pine,

looking at Mt. Whitney —
the mountain she loved, had climbed
on her birthday so many times.
But the dying leave

before the last breath.
She would not have seen
the stone angel —
Nor would she need to,

my mother, ninety,
in a deepening coma,
on the steep switchbacks
with my father —

Then, before all motion
stopped: she lifted her arm
and reached for his hand,
to help her cross the last stream.

SPIRIT HORSES

August, in Vermont,
I saw mist swiftly rise,
white horses from a black

forest pond —
Rearing like a rush of breath,
they rose

straight up,
then veered
toward an unseen shore.

From stillness to stillness
they sped, spirit horses
free from all weight,

a star-braided mare
calling to them
from the other side.

In the mirror of the night I saw
I too was a ghost, although
still flesh, leaf-deep in the now.

But the horses, as they
disappeared, in silence called.
And I knew that soon

I'd lay my head along
my spirit horse's fluent neck,
hold on to the imagined mane —

Still I wavered: drop my
rags, my chores? I said,
I'm growing old. Then her

voice, star-deep in the night:
But without wanting
the highest, is it really life?

MY PARENTS FLIRTING

"Excuse me, Ma'am," my father
would glance at my mother
in that sidelong way —
"but haven't we met before?"

— "No Sir, you must be
mistaken. I haven't had the honor."
He'd persist: "Madam, are you not
the beautiful brunette I saw

at the teahouse near Jastarnia Harbor,
that July when we were young?"
"So sorry Sir. That sunlit lady wasn't me."
"Then it must have been a dream:

the sea exceptionally blue, and you
stepping out on the white terrace . . ."
Slowly she'd lift the veil: "Now I
remember! It's you!" — "It's me!"

And they'd fall into each other's arms;
resume the marriage like a stroll
into autumn, the years like leaves
around their rustling feet.

The leaves persist with wooing;
the leaves do not believe
this man and woman are now gone,
two syllables of eternity.

If we continue, at least as echoes,
perhaps this is the game
my parents still play.
Clothed with the fractals

of sun and sea, she leans
toward him: "Pardon me . . .
but haven't we met
before?"

FOR AMELIA EARHART
Yosemite

The year of the heavy snowmelt,
waterfalls were a rush of white,
pure movement leaning on air.
The water pulsed, a liquid light

overleaping mountains.
The wind blew sideways
curtains of mist.
I was drenched, I slid

on wet stones, each stone
shone *go, don't*
ask what is ahead —
Now I no longer know

choice from gravity,
there is no breath
except the shearing air.
To lose the ground

is not a metaphor
here on the glistening
granite, and here is how
I go: along the ledge

of nothing, grasping
at thin branches — the spray
beating so high, I need
a mother in the sky —

and in your
leather cap, you wave.

ABOUT THE AUTHOR

Oriana Ivy was born and raised in Poland. She came to the United States when she was 17. Her poems, essays, book reviews, and translations have been published in *Poetry*, *Ploughshares*, *Best American Poetry*, *Nimrod*, *Spoon River Review*, *The Iowa Review*, *Black Warrior Review*, *Los Angeles Review of Books*, and many others. She's the prize winning author of the chapbooks *April Snow* (Finishing Line Press) and *From a New World* (Paper Nautilus). A former journalist and community college instructor, she leads an online Poetry Salon. Her poetry-and-culture blog, oriana-poetry.blogspot.com, has gained an international audience. She lives in Southern California.